The Smart Home Revolution:
Transforming Your Living Space

By

Jerry J. Martin

TABLE OF CONTENTS

CHAPTER I
Introduction

A. Importance of the home environment

In today's fast-paced world, our homes serve as our sanctuaries, providing a space of comfort, security, and personal expression. The home environment plays a crucial role in shaping our well-being and quality of life. It is where we seek refuge from the outside world, relax, and spend time with loved ones. With the advent of smart home technology, the concept of a home has been revolutionized, offering a whole new level of convenience, efficiency, and control.

The importance of the home environment cannot be overstated. It is where we recharge our energy, nurture relationships, and create lasting memories. Our homes reflect our personalities, tastes, and lifestyles, and they should be tailored to meet our individual needs and desires. A well-designed home environment enhances our overall happiness, productivity, and satisfaction.

Smart home technology has emerged as a transformative force in this regard. It offers an unprecedented level of connectivity and automation, enabling us to seamlessly control and manage various aspects of our homes. From adjusting the lighting and temperature to monitoring security cameras and even remotely managing appliances, smart homes empower us to have complete command over our living spaces.

Moreover, the importance of the home environment extends beyond personal benefits. Smart homes are also instrumental in promoting sustainability and energy efficiency. By optimizing energy consumption, automating systems, and integrating renewable energy sources, smart homes contribute to a greener and more eco-friendly future.

The Smart Home Revolution: Transforming Your Living Space aims to explore the potential of smart home technology and its impact on our lives. It will guide readers in understanding the intricacies of smart home systems, selecting appropriate devices, and implementing them effectively. By embracing the smart home revolution, readers can transform their living spaces into intelligent and personalized environments that enhance comfort, convenience, and well-being. Get ready to embark on a journey of discovery as we delve into the fascinating world of smart homes and witness the transformative power they hold.

B. Rise of smart home technology

The past decade has witnessed an exponential rise in smart home technology, revolutionizing the way we interact with our living spaces. With the rapid advancement of Internet of Things (IoT) and artificial intelligence, our homes have become smarter, more connected, and increasingly responsive to our needs. This rise of smart home technology has paved the way for a new era in home automation, transforming the way we live, work, and interact within our domestic environments.

The proliferation of smart devices and their integration into our homes has been a game-changer. From voice-activated assistants to smart thermostats, security systems, lighting, and entertainment systems, our homes are evolving into intelligent ecosystems. This shift is fueled by the increasing affordability, accessibility, and convenience of smart home products, making them more attainable for everyday consumers.

The rise of smart home technology can be attributed to several factors. First and foremost, the desire for convenience and efficiency has been a driving force behind the adoption of smart home devices. With just a few taps on a smartphone or a simple voice command, we can now control and automate various aspects of our homes, saving time and effort. Whether it's adjusting the temperature, turning off lights, or even preheating the oven on our way back from work, smart homes offer unparalleled convenience and remote accessibility.

Another significant factor contributing to the rise of smart home technology is the growing awareness of energy conservation and sustainability. Smart thermostats, for example, can learn our preferences, adapt to our schedules, and optimize energy usage, reducing our carbon footprint and saving on utility bills. This eco-conscious approach resonates with a generation that values sustainability and strives to make a positive impact on the environment.

Furthermore, the rise of smart home technology is also propelled by the rapid advancement of connectivity and networking infrastructure. With the widespread availability of high-speed internet and the proliferation of wireless communication protocols, our homes can now be seamlessly interconnected, enabling seamless integration of various devices and systems. This interconnectedness creates a holistic ecosystem where smart devices collaborate and communicate with each other, enhancing the overall functionality and user experience.

The Smart Home Revolution: Transforming Your Living Space seeks to shed light on the rising tide of smart home technology and its transformative potential. By exploring the various devices, systems, and integration possibilities, this book aims to empower readers to embrace the smart home revolution and unlock the full potential of their living spaces. Get ready to embark on a journey into the exciting world of smart homes and witness how this technology is reshaping the way we live and interact within our homes.

C. Purpose of the book

The purpose of The Smart Home Revolution: Transforming Your Living Space is to serve as a comprehensive guide and resource for readers who are curious about smart home technology and eager to embark on their own journey of transforming their living spaces. In an era where technology is increasingly integrated into every aspect of our lives, this book aims to demystify the world of smart homes, providing practical insights, tips, and recommendations for creating a smart home environment that is tailored to individual needs and preferences.

With the abundance of smart home devices available in the market, it can be overwhelming for readers to navigate through the myriad of options and make informed decisions. The purpose of this book is to streamline that process, offering guidance on assessing current living spaces, planning and budgeting for a smart home setup, and selecting the most suitable devices and systems for specific requirements.

Additionally, the book aims to dispel common misconceptions and myths surrounding smart home technology. It provides clarity on what a smart home truly entails, discussing the essential components, benefits, and advantages. By understanding the foundations of smart homes, readers can make informed choices and avoid potential pitfalls.

Another crucial purpose of this book is to delve into the practical aspects of smart home integration. It offers insights into connecting devices and creating a network within the home, exploring the role of smart home hubs and controllers, and addressing interoperability and compatibility considerations. Armed with this knowledge, readers can build a seamless and efficient smart home ecosystem that suits their lifestyle and preferences.

Moreover, this book explores the various ways in which smart homes can transform living spaces. It delves into the realm of smart lighting and ambiance control, discussing how lighting can be personalized and automated to create the perfect atmosphere. It also examines energy efficiency and the role of smart thermostats in optimizing comfort while reducing energy consumption. Additionally, the book covers home security and surveillance systems, empowering readers to enhance the safety and security of their homes.

Furthermore, the book delves into the aspects of comfort and convenience that smart homes offer. It explores the world of voice assistants and smart speakers, showcasing how these devices can become valuable companions in our daily lives. It also discusses smart appliances and automated routines that can simplify tasks and streamline daily routines. Additionally, it delves into entertainment systems and media integration, highlighting how smart homes can elevate the overall entertainment experience.

Ultimately, The Smart Home Revolution: Transforming Your Living Space aims to equip readers with the knowledge, insights, and inspiration to embrace the smart home revolution. It looks into the future of smart homes, discussing emerging technologies, trends, and potential challenges. By the end of this book, readers will be empowered to create a smart home environment that truly transforms their living spaces, enhancing comfort, convenience, and well-being. Get ready to embark on an exciting journey into the world of smart homes and witness the endless possibilities that lie within your reach.

CHAPTER II
Understanding Smart Homes

A. Definition and components of a smart home

In order to fully grasp the concept of a smart home, it is essential to understand its definition and the key components that make it a reality. At its core, a smart home is a residential space equipped with devices and systems that are interconnected and can be controlled and automated through a central hub or remotely via a smartphone or other smart devices.

The components of a smart home encompass a wide range of devices and systems that work together to enhance comfort, convenience, and efficiency. One of the fundamental components is smart lighting, which allows users to control and adjust the lighting intensity, color, and schedule, either manually or through automated routines. This not only provides personalized lighting experiences but also helps in energy conservation.

Another crucial aspect of a smart home is climate control, typically facilitated by a smart thermostat. Smart thermostats enable users to remotely control and program temperature settings, adapting to individual preferences and schedules. These devices also often incorporate learning algorithms that analyze usage patterns to optimize energy consumption and reduce utility costs.

Security and surveillance systems are essential components of a smart home, providing homeowners with peace of mind and enhanced protection. These systems can include smart door locks, motion sensors, surveillance cameras, and alarm systems that can be monitored and controlled remotely. Integration with smartphone apps enables users to receive real-time alerts and access live video feeds, adding an extra layer of security to their homes.

Entertainment systems also play a significant role in smart homes, transforming the way we enjoy media content. From smart TVs with streaming capabilities to wireless speakers and home theater systems, these devices can be seamlessly integrated into the smart home ecosystem, offering immersive audiovisual experiences that can be controlled from a central hub or smart devices.

In addition to these core components, smart homes often incorporate other devices and systems such as smart appliances (e.g., refrigerators, washing machines) that can be remotely monitored and controlled, voice assistants (e.g., Amazon Alexa, Google Assistant) that enable voice commands for various tasks, and even automated routines that can synchronize different devices to perform specific actions.

The beauty of a smart home lies in its interconnectedness and the ability to control and automate various aspects of the living space. By leveraging the power of technology, homeowners can create personalized environments that adapt to their needs and preferences, offering convenience, energy efficiency, and improved quality of life.

In the subsequent sections of this book, we will explore in greater detail the benefits, misconceptions, and considerations related to smart home technology. By gaining a comprehensive understanding of smart homes, readers will be well-equipped to embark on their own journey of transforming their living spaces. Get ready to unlock the potential of smart home technology and discover a new level of comfort and convenience.

B. Benefits and advantages of smart home technology

Smart home technology offers a multitude of benefits and advantages that can greatly enhance the way we live and interact with our living spaces. From convenience and energy efficiency to increased safety and comfort, the advantages of smart homes are compelling reasons to embrace this transformative technology.

One of the key benefits of smart homes is the unparalleled convenience they provide. With smart home devices, controlling and managing various aspects of the home becomes effortless. Imagine being able to adjust the thermostat, turn on/off lights, lock doors, or even start appliances with a simple voice command or a few taps on a smartphone. Smart homes eliminate the need for manual intervention and streamline daily tasks, saving time and effort.

Energy efficiency is another significant advantage of smart home technology. With smart thermostats, for example, homeowners can optimize temperature settings based on occupancy and personal preferences. These devices can learn usage patterns and adjust the temperature automatically, resulting in energy savings and reduced utility bills. Similarly, smart lighting systems can be programmed to turn on/off or dim according to occupancy and natural light, maximizing energy conservation.

Smart homes also offer enhanced safety and security features. With the integration of smart locks, motion sensors, and surveillance cameras, homeowners can monitor and control their homes remotely. Real-time notifications can alert them to potential security breaches or suspicious activities, providing peace of mind even when away. The ability to remotely lock doors or view live video feeds adds an extra layer of protection to the home.

Comfort and personalization are significant advantages of smart homes. With the ability to customize lighting, temperature, and even entertainment settings, homeowners can create the perfect ambiance for any occasion. Imagine arriving home to a well-lit, comfortably cooled environment or waking up to the gentle transition of lighting and music. Smart homes empower individuals to tailor their living spaces to their preferences, enhancing comfort and creating a more enjoyable atmosphere.

Moreover, smart homes contribute to a more sustainable and eco-friendly lifestyle. By optimizing energy consumption and reducing waste, smart home devices help conserve valuable resources and minimize the environmental impact. The ability to monitor energy usage and make informed decisions about energy-intensive appliances or systems empowers homeowners to live in a more environmentally conscious manner.

Accessibility is yet another advantage of smart homes. Individuals with mobility challenges or disabilities can greatly benefit from the automation and remote control features. Smart home technology enables them to control their environment independently, improving their quality of life and fostering greater autonomy.

The benefits and advantages of smart home technology are multifaceted, making it an appealing choice for homeowners seeking to enhance their living spaces. The subsequent sections of this book will delve deeper into the practical aspects of implementing and integrating smart home devices and systems, enabling readers to unlock the full potential of this transformative technology. Get ready to embrace the benefits of smart homes and experience a new level of convenience, energy efficiency, safety, and comfort within your living space.

C. Common misconceptions about smart homes

Despite the growing popularity and advancements in smart home technology, there are still several misconceptions that surround the concept of smart homes. These misconceptions often stem from limited understanding or outdated information. By debunking these myths, we can gain a clearer understanding of what smart homes truly entail.

One common misconception is that smart homes are only for tech-savvy individuals or early adopters. In reality, smart home technology has become increasingly user-friendly and accessible to people of all technological backgrounds. Many smart devices are designed with intuitive interfaces and can be easily controlled through smartphone apps or voice commands. Setting up a smart home doesn't require extensive technical expertise but rather a willingness to explore and learn.

Another misconception is that smart homes are expensive and only affordable for the affluent. While it is true that some high-end smart home systems can come with a hefty price tag, there are also numerous affordable options available in the market. The cost of smart home devices has significantly decreased over the years, making them more accessible to a wider range of consumers. Additionally, building a smart home can be done gradually, starting with a few key devices and expanding over time based on individual budgets and priorities.

Privacy and security concerns are often associated with smart homes. Some people worry that having interconnected devices may compromise their personal data or make their homes vulnerable to hacking. While it's essential to take precautions and ensure proper security measures are in place, it's worth noting that smart home technology has made significant strides in improving privacy and security features. Manufacturers are implementing robust encryption protocols, two-factor authentication, and regular software updates to address these concerns.

Another misconception is that smart homes are only focused on luxury and convenience, lacking practical benefits. However, smart home technology offers numerous practical advantages beyond mere convenience. For example, energy-saving features and automation capabilities can lead to significant cost savings on utility bills. Smart home systems can also enhance safety and security, providing real-time notifications and remote monitoring capabilities. Moreover, smart home devices can cater to specific needs, such as providing accessibility features for individuals with disabilities or elderly individuals.

Additionally, some people believe that once a smart home is set up, it requires constant maintenance and troubleshooting. While it's true that occasional updates and troubleshooting may be necessary, smart home devices are designed to be user-friendly and reliable. Manufacturers often provide user support and regular software updates to improve performance and address any issues that may arise. With proper setup and maintenance, smart homes can offer a seamless and hassle-free experience.

By dispelling these common misconceptions, readers can develop a more accurate understanding of smart homes and their potential benefits. The subsequent sections of this book will delve into practical guidance and insights, empowering readers to embrace smart home technology confidently. Get ready to challenge these misconceptions and unlock the true potential of smart homes as we transform our living spaces into intelligent, efficient, and personalized environments.

CHAPTER III
Getting Started with Smart Home Technology

A. Assessing your current living space

Before diving into the world of smart home technology, it is crucial to assess your current living space to determine its compatibility and specific needs. This assessment will help you make informed decisions about which smart home devices and systems will be most suitable for your home.

Start by identifying the areas of your home that could benefit from smart home technology. Consider the rooms or spaces where you spend the most time or where automation and control would be most valuable. Common areas to consider include the living room, bedroom, kitchen, and outdoor spaces.

Next, evaluate your existing infrastructure and connectivity. Assess the availability and quality of your Wi-Fi network, as a stable internet connection is essential for seamless communication between smart devices.

Determine the strength of the signal in different areas of your home, including any potential dead zones or areas with poor connectivity.

Take stock of your electrical system as well. Check the number of available electrical outlets and consider whether additional outlets or power strips may be required to accommodate smart devices. Also, consider the wiring in your home, as certain smart devices may require specific electrical considerations.

It is also important to consider the compatibility of your current devices and systems with smart home technology. Review the appliances, electronics, and systems you already have in your home. Determine whether they can be integrated or upgraded to work within a smart home ecosystem. For example, if you have a home security system, check if it can be connected to a smart home hub or if it requires specific smart home-compatible components.

Additionally, assess your personal preferences and lifestyle. Think about your priorities when it comes to convenience, energy efficiency, security, or entertainment. Consider the routines and habits of your household members, as well as any specific needs or preferences that should be addressed through smart home technology.

Finally, establish a budget for your smart home setup. Determine how much you are willing to invest in smart home devices and systems. Keep in mind that building a smart home can be done incrementally, starting with a few key devices and expanding over time. Setting a budget will help you prioritize and make informed decisions when selecting smart home products.

By thoroughly assessing your current living space, infrastructure, compatibility, and personal preferences, you will be better equipped to embark on your smart home journey. The subsequent sections of this book will guide you through the planning, selection, and implementation of smart home devices and systems, empowering you to create a customized and efficient smart home environment. Get ready to transform your living space into a smart home that caters to your unique needs and enhances your daily life.

B. Planning and budgeting for a smart home setup

Planning and budgeting are essential steps when venturing into the world of smart home technology. Careful consideration of your needs, priorities, and financial resources will help you create a well-designed and cost-effective smart home setup that aligns with your goals.

Begin by defining your smart home objectives. Determine what you hope to achieve with your smart home setup. Do you prioritize convenience, energy efficiency, security, or a combination of factors? Understanding your goals will guide your planning process and help you make informed decisions when selecting smart devices and systems.

Next, create a list of the specific smart home devices and systems you would like to incorporate. Consider the components mentioned in the outline, such as smart lighting, thermostats, security systems, entertainment systems, and appliances. Research different options available in the market and compare their features, functionality, and compatibility with your existing infrastructure.

With your list of desired smart home devices in hand, it's time to create a budget. Determine the maximum amount you are willing to invest in your smart home setup. Take into account the cost of individual devices, installation expenses, and any additional accessories or services that may be required. Remember to allocate a portion of your budget for potential future expansions or upgrades.

Prioritize your smart home investments based on your budget and goals. Identify the devices or systems that are crucial for your initial setup and those that can be added later. This approach allows you to build your smart home gradually and prevents overspending on unnecessary items.

Research promotions, discounts, and package deals that may be available for smart home devices. Look for reputable brands that offer quality products at competitive prices. Consider reading customer reviews and seeking recommendations to ensure you make well-informed choices.

When budgeting, don't forget to account for installation and setup costs. Depending on the complexity of the devices and your technical expertise, you may need professional assistance to ensure proper installation and integration. Factor in these costs when planning your budget.

Lastly, keep in mind the long-term cost savings that can be achieved with a smart home setup. While there may be an upfront investment, smart devices can contribute to energy efficiency, resulting in lower utility bills over time. Consider the potential return on investment in terms of energy savings, increased property value, and enhanced convenience.

By carefully planning and budgeting for your smart home setup, you can make informed decisions and ensure that your investment aligns with your goals and financial capabilities. The subsequent sections of this book will provide guidance on device selection, integration, and implementation, helping you create a smart home environment that maximizes value and enhances your lifestyle. Get ready to embark on a well-planned and budget-conscious smart home journey.

C. Choosing the right devices and systems

Choosing the right devices and systems is a crucial step in building an effective and functional smart home. With a multitude of options available in the market, it's essential to consider factors such as compatibility, features, reliability, and user experience when making your selections.

Start by reviewing the list of desired smart home devices and systems you created during the planning phase. Consider the specific features and functionalities that are important to you. For example, if energy efficiency is a priority, look for smart thermostats with advanced scheduling capabilities or energy monitoring features. If home security is a concern, prioritize devices such as smart locks, security cameras, or motion sensors.

Research different brands and manufacturers to ensure that the devices you choose are reputable and reliable. Look for product reviews, customer feedback, and expert opinions to gauge the performance and durability of the devices. Consider factors such as ease of use, compatibility with other devices, and availability of customer support.

Compatibility is a critical aspect to consider when selecting smart home devices. Ensure that the devices you choose can integrate and communicate with each other seamlessly. Look for compatibility with common smart home protocols and platforms such as Zigbee, Z-Wave, or Wi-Fi. Compatibility ensures that your devices can work together in a cohesive ecosystem, maximizing the benefits of your smart home setup.

Consider the scalability of the devices and systems you choose. Smart home technology is constantly evolving, and it's important to select devices that can grow with your needs. Look for systems that offer expansion options, allowing you to add more devices or integrate with new technologies in the future. This scalability ensures that your smart home setup remains future-proof and adaptable.

When choosing smart home devices, take into account your personal preferences and user experience. Consider the user interfaces, control options, and automation capabilities of the devices. Some devices may offer intuitive smartphone apps, while others may have voice control or physical interfaces. Choose devices that align with your preferred method of control and provide a user-friendly experience.

Additionally, consider the aesthetics and design of the devices. Since smart home devices are often visible in your living space, their appearance should complement your home decor and personal style. Look for devices that offer various color options or customizable finishes to ensure a seamless integration into your existing environment.

Finally, take into account the budget you established during the planning phase. Compare prices, features, and performance to find the best value for your investment. Remember that higher price does not always guarantee superior quality, so make sure to weigh the features and reliability against the cost.

By carefully considering compatibility, features, reliability, user experience, scalability, and budget, you can choose the right devices and systems for your smart home setup. The subsequent sections of this book will delve into specific device categories, offering insights and recommendations to help you make informed decisions. Get ready to select the perfect devices that will transform your living space into a truly intelligent and efficient smart home.

CHAPTER IV
Smart Home Integration

A. Connecting devices and creating a network

Smart home integration is the process of connecting and synchronizing various devices within your smart home ecosystem. Creating a network of interconnected devices allows for seamless communication and coordination, enabling you to control and automate multiple aspects of your living space.

Start by establishing a central hub or controller for your smart home. This hub serves as the command center that connects and manages all the devices in your network. There are various options available, ranging from standalone smart home hubs to voice-activated assistants like Amazon Alexa or Google Assistant. Choose a hub that is compatible with your devices and offers the features and functionalities you desire.

Next, connect your smart home devices to the hub or controller. Depending on the device and technology used, this can be done via Wi-Fi, Bluetooth, Zigbee,

Z-Wave, or a combination of these protocols. Each device will have its own setup process, which typically involves following the manufacturer's instructions and using a dedicated app to establish the connection. The app will guide you through the steps of connecting the device to your network and linking it to the central hub.

Ensure that all devices are connected to the same network and operating on compatible frequencies or protocols. This allows for smooth communication and ensures that the devices can interact with each other effectively. Most smart home hubs or controllers have dedicated companion apps that help manage the network and facilitate the connection process.

Once your devices are connected, explore the capabilities of the hub or controller to create automation routines and customizations. These routines allow you to program specific actions or behaviors based on triggers or schedules. For example, you can set up a routine that automatically turns on the lights and adjusts the thermostat when you arrive home. Or you can create a routine that gradually dims the lights and plays relaxing music as you wind down for the night.

Consider grouping devices into rooms or zones to simplify control and organization. This grouping allows you to control multiple devices simultaneously with a single command. For example, you can create a group called "Living Room" that includes the smart TV, speakers, and lights in that area. This way, you can turn on/off or adjust all the devices in the living room at once.

As you integrate your devices, it's important to periodically check for firmware updates and ensure that your devices are running the latest software versions. These updates often include bug fixes, security patches, and new features, ensuring optimal performance and compatibility.

Smart home integration is a dynamic and ongoing process. As you expand your smart home ecosystem or add new devices, it's important to revisit the integration process and ensure all devices are connected and working together seamlessly. Regularly review and adjust automation routines and settings to optimize your smart home experience.

By connecting devices and creating a network within your smart home, you can unleash the full potential of automation and control. The subsequent sections of this book will delve into specific device categories and explore how they can be integrated into your smart home ecosystem. Get ready to experience the power of interconnected devices as you transform your living space into a truly intelligent and responsive environment.

B. Smart home hubs and controllers

Smart home hubs and controllers play a crucial role in the integration and management of devices within your smart home ecosystem. These central devices serve as the control center, allowing you to connect and control a wide range of smart devices from a single interface. Understanding the capabilities and features of smart home hubs and controllers is essential for optimizing your smart home experience.

There are several options available when it comes to choosing a smart home hub or controller. One popular choice is a standalone smart home hub, specifically designed to connect and control various devices within your smart home. These hubs typically support multiple protocols such as Wi-Fi, Zigbee, and Z-Wave, allowing for seamless integration with a wide range of smart devices. They often come with companion apps that provide a user-friendly interface for managing devices, creating automation routines, and monitoring the status of your smart home.

Another type of smart home hub is the voice-activated assistant, such as Amazon Alexa or Google Assistant. These devices not only serve as hubs but also offer the added convenience of voice control. With a voice-activated assistant, you can issue commands and control your smart home devices using natural language. These assistants can perform a wide range of tasks, from adjusting the lighting and temperature to playing music and answering questions. They can also integrate with other smart devices and services, expanding the functionality of your smart home.

When selecting a smart home hub or controller, compatibility is a crucial consideration. Ensure that the hub supports the communication protocols used by your smart devices. Compatibility ensures that all devices can seamlessly connect and interact with each other, allowing for a cohesive smart home experience. Additionally, check whether the hub integrates with popular smart home platforms and services, as this can enhance the versatility and expandability of your smart home ecosystem.

Ease of use and user interface are important factors to consider as well. Look for hubs or controllers with intuitive and user-friendly interfaces that make it easy to manage and control your smart home devices. A well-designed app or interface will simplify the setup process, allow for effortless device management, and provide the flexibility to customize automation routines and schedules according to your preferences.

Another aspect to consider is the scalability of the hub or controller. As your smart home expands, you may add more devices and systems. Ensure that the hub you choose can accommodate future additions and integrates well with a wide range of devices. This scalability allows for a seamless expansion of your smart home without having to replace the entire hub or controller.

Finally, take into account the overall reliability and customer support provided by the manufacturer. Look for hubs or controllers from reputable brands that have a track record of delivering quality products and providing timely software updates. Customer support is crucial in case you encounter any issues or have questions during the setup and operation of your smart home.

By selecting the right smart home hub or controller, you can centralize the management and control of your smart devices, simplifying the integration process and enhancing the overall functionality of your smart home. The subsequent sections of this book will delve into specific device categories, exploring how they can be integrated into your smart home ecosystem using hubs or controllers. Get ready to take control of your smart home and unlock the true potential of automation and convenience.

C. Choosing the right devices and systems

Choosing the right devices and systems is a crucial step in building an effective and functional smart home. With a multitude of options available in the market, it's essential to consider factors such as compatibility, features, reliability, and user experience when making your selections.

Start by reviewing the list of desired smart home devices and systems you created during the planning phase. Consider the specific features and functionalities that are important to you. For example, if energy efficiency is a priority, look for smart thermostats with advanced scheduling capabilities or energy monitoring features. If home security is a concern, prioritize devices such as smart locks, security cameras, or motion sensors.

Research different brands and manufacturers to ensure that the devices you choose are reputable and reliable. Look for product reviews, customer feedback, and expert opinions to gauge the performance and durability of the devices. Consider factors such as ease of use, compatibility with other devices, and availability of customer support.

Compatibility is a critical aspect to consider when selecting smart home devices. Ensure that the devices you choose can integrate and communicate with each other seamlessly. Look for compatibility with common smart home protocols and platforms such as Zigbee, Z-Wave, or Wi-Fi. Compatibility ensures that your devices can work together in a cohesive ecosystem, maximizing the benefits of your smart home setup.

Consider the scalability of the devices and systems you choose. Smart home technology is constantly evolving, and it's important to select devices that can grow with your needs. Look for systems that offer expansion options, allowing you to add more devices or integrate with new technologies in the future. This scalability ensures that your smart home setup remains future-proof and adaptable.

When choosing smart home devices, take into account your personal preferences and user experience. Consider the user interfaces, control options, and automation capabilities of the devices. Some devices may offer intuitive smartphone apps, while others may have voice control or physical interfaces. Choose devices that align with your preferred method of control and provide a user-friendly experience.

Additionally, consider the aesthetics and design of the devices. Since smart home devices are often visible in your living space, their appearance should complement your home decor and personal style. Look for devices that offer various color options or customizable finishes to ensure a seamless integration into your existing environment.

Finally, take into account the budget you established during the planning phase. Compare prices, features, and performance to find the best value for your investment.

Remember that higher price does not always guarantee superior quality, so make sure to weigh the features and reliability against the cost.

By carefully considering compatibility, features, reliability, user experience, scalability, and budget, you can choose the right devices and systems for your smart home setup. The subsequent sections of this book will delve into specific device categories, offering insights and recommendations to help you make informed decisions. Get ready to select the perfect devices that will transform your living space into a truly intelligent and efficient smart home.

CHAPTER V
Transforming Living Spaces

A. Smart lighting and ambiance control

Smart lighting is one of the key components that can truly transform the atmosphere and ambiance of your living spaces. With the ability to control lighting intensity, color, and scheduling, smart lighting allows you to create personalized and dynamic environments that suit your mood, activities, or even the time of day.

One of the primary benefits of smart lighting is the convenience and flexibility it offers. With smart bulbs or lighting systems, you can easily adjust the lighting settings with a few taps on your smartphone or through voice commands. No more getting up to switch off lights or fumbling for switches in the dark. Smart lighting puts you in complete control, allowing you to effortlessly create the perfect lighting scene for any occasion.

Smart lighting also enhances energy efficiency by providing greater control over usage. You can set up schedules or automation routines that turn off lights when not needed or adjust brightness levels based on natural light conditions. This intelligent management helps reduce energy consumption and lower electricity bills. Some smart lighting systems even offer features like motion sensors or daylight harvesting, further optimizing energy efficiency.

Furthermore, smart lighting allows for customization and personalization. You can choose from a wide spectrum of colors and shades to set the desired mood or create a specific ambiance. Whether you want a cozy warm glow for relaxation, vibrant colors for a party, or cool lighting for focus and productivity, smart lighting can adapt to your preferences and transform the atmosphere of any space.

Integration with other smart home devices and systems enhances the capabilities of smart lighting. For example, you can synchronize your lighting with other devices such as smart speakers or entertainment systems to create immersive experiences. Imagine watching a movie and having your lights dim automatically to create a cinematic atmosphere. Or having your lights gradually brighten in the morning to simulate a natural sunrise, gently waking you up.

Smart lighting can also contribute to home security and safety. You can program lighting routines that simulate occupancy when you're away, giving the impression that someone is home. This can act as a deterrent against potential intruders. Additionally, you can set up motion-activated lighting in areas such as hallways or staircases, providing enhanced safety and visibility during nighttime.

The ease of installation and setup is another advantage of smart lighting. Many smart bulbs can be easily replaced with existing traditional bulbs, requiring no rewiring or complex installation processes. Some bulbs even connect directly to your Wi-Fi network, eliminating the need for additional hubs or controllers.

By incorporating smart lighting into your smart home setup, you can truly transform the ambiance and mood of your living spaces. The subsequent sections of this book will explore other aspects of transforming living spaces, delving into additional device categories and their integration within a smart home ecosystem. Get ready to unleash the power of smart lighting and create breathtaking environments that elevate your living experience.

B. Energy efficiency and smart thermostats

Energy efficiency is a crucial aspect of transforming living spaces, and smart thermostats are powerful tools that can help you optimize energy usage and create a more sustainable home environment. Smart thermostats provide advanced features and intelligent control over your heating and cooling systems, enabling you to save energy and reduce utility costs.

One of the primary benefits of smart thermostats is their ability to learn and adapt to your lifestyle and preferences. These devices employ advanced algorithms and machine learning capabilities to analyze your patterns of temperature adjustments and create customized schedules. Over time, they learn your temperature preferences for different times of the day and automatically adjust the settings to maximize comfort while minimizing energy waste.

With smart thermostats, you can remotely control your heating and cooling systems from anywhere using a smartphone app or through voice commands. This allows you to adjust the temperature before you arrive home, ensuring a comfortable environment upon your arrival while avoiding unnecessary energy consumption when no one is home. The ability to control your thermostat remotely also means that you can make adjustments even when you're away, helping to conserve energy when unexpected circumstances arise.

Another key feature of smart thermostats is their ability to integrate with external factors such as weather forecasts and occupancy sensors. By considering external conditions, smart thermostats can optimize temperature settings for maximum energy efficiency. For example, on a hot summer day, a smart thermostat can adjust the cooling system to work more efficiently and reduce energy usage during peak demand hours.

Smart thermostats often come with energy monitoring features that provide real-time data and insights on your energy usage. You can track your energy consumption patterns, identify trends, and make informed decisions to further optimize efficiency. Some smart thermostats also provide energy-saving tips and recommendations based on your usage patterns, empowering you to make smarter choices to reduce energy waste.

Integration with other smart home devices and systems enhances the capabilities of smart thermostats. For instance, you can synchronize your thermostat with smart lighting systems to adjust lighting levels based on occupancy or natural light conditions. This coordination ensures that energy is used efficiently and helps create a cohesive smart home ecosystem.

Additionally, many utility companies offer incentives and programs for using smart thermostats. These programs may include discounted energy rates or rebates for installing and using energy-efficient devices. By participating in such programs, you can not only save on energy costs but also contribute to a more sustainable energy grid.

The installation and setup process for smart thermostats can vary depending on the model and your existing heating and cooling systems. It's advisable to consult professional installers or follow the manufacturer's instructions for proper installation. Many manufacturers provide detailed guidance and support to ensure a smooth setup process.

By incorporating smart thermostats into your smart home setup, you can significantly improve energy efficiency and reduce your environmental footprint. The subsequent sections of this book will explore other aspects of transforming living spaces, delving into additional device categories and their integration within a smart home ecosystem. Get ready to revolutionize your living spaces with smart thermostats and experience a more comfortable, energy-efficient, and sustainable home environment.

C. Home security and surveillance systems

When it comes to transforming living spaces, ensuring the safety and security of your home is paramount. Smart home security and surveillance systems provide advanced features and peace of mind, allowing you to monitor and protect your home even when you're away.

One of the key components of a smart home security system is surveillance cameras. These cameras, equipped with high-resolution video capabilities, enable you to monitor different areas of your home both indoors and outdoors. With smart cameras, you can view live feeds or recorded footage remotely through smartphone apps or dedicated monitoring interfaces. This constant visibility acts as a deterrent to potential intruders and provides valuable evidence in case of any security incidents.

Smart surveillance systems often include motion sensors that can trigger alerts or recordings when movement is detected. These sensors can be strategically placed in areas of concern, such as entrances, windows, or sensitive locations within your home. When activated, they can send notifications to your smartphone, allowing you to promptly respond to potential threats or unusual activities.

Integration with other smart home devices enhances the security capabilities of your home. For example, you can link your surveillance system with smart lighting to create an illusion of occupancy when you're away. This automation, along with other security features such as smart locks, can contribute to a comprehensive and layered security approach.

Smart home security systems also offer convenient features like remote access and control. With remote access, you can arm or disarm your security system, lock or unlock doors, and view live camera feeds from anywhere using your smartphone or other internet-connected devices. This level of control ensures that you can monitor and secure your home, even when you're not physically present.

Many smart home security systems provide additional features like two-way audio communication. This enables you to communicate with visitors or potential intruders remotely through built-in speakers and microphones. Whether you're checking in on a delivery person or warning an intruder that the authorities have been notified, this feature adds an extra layer of protection and control.

Cloud storage and video playback options are common features of smart home security systems. Recorded footage from surveillance cameras can be stored securely in the cloud, eliminating the need for physical storage devices and providing convenient access to historical data. Some systems offer advanced video analytics that can detect and highlight specific events or movements within the recorded footage, making it easier to review and analyze security-related incidents.

Installation of a smart home security system may require professional assistance, especially if it involves complex wiring or integration with existing security infrastructure. Consult with experts or follow the manufacturer's instructions to ensure a proper setup that meets your specific security needs.

By incorporating smart home security and surveillance systems, you can protect your home, loved ones, and belongings with advanced features and remote accessibility. The subsequent sections of this book will explore other aspects of transforming living spaces, delving into additional device categories and their integration within a smart home ecosystem. Get ready to enhance the security of your living spaces and experience a greater sense of safety and control within your smart home.

CHAPTER VI
Enhancing Comfort and Convenience

A. Voice assistants and smart speakers

Voice assistants and smart speakers have revolutionized the way we interact with our homes, offering unparalleled convenience and control. These intelligent devices, powered by artificial intelligence, can understand and respond to voice commands, allowing you to access information, control smart devices, and enjoy a wide range of entertainment options.

One of the key features of voice assistants is their ability to provide hands-free control over your smart home devices. With a simple voice command, you can turn on/off lights, adjust thermostats, lock doors, play music, or even order groceries. Voice assistants such as Amazon Alexa, Google Assistant, and Apple Siri have become the central command centers of many smart homes, enabling effortless control and automation.

Smart speakers, equipped with voice assistants, act as the hub for these voice-activated capabilities. These speakers not only deliver high-quality audio but also serve as the gateway to the vast array of features offered by voice assistants. They can play your favorite music, stream podcasts, provide weather updates, answer questions, and even control compatible smart devices throughout your home.

The integration of voice assistants with smart home devices allows for seamless control through natural language. Instead of having to interact with multiple apps or physical controls, you can simply speak commands or questions aloud, and the voice assistant will respond accordingly. This hands-free control enhances convenience and accessibility, particularly for individuals with mobility challenges or those who prefer a more intuitive way of interacting with technology.

Voice assistants also excel at providing personalized experiences and information. Through voice recognition technology, they can distinguish between different users and tailor responses and recommendations accordingly. This means that each member of your household can access their personalized music playlists, receive tailored news updates, or have their individual preferences catered to.

In addition to controlling smart home devices, voice assistants can integrate with a wide range of services and platforms, expanding their functionality. You can use voice commands to request rideshare services, order food delivery, check your calendar, set reminders, or even make hands-free phone calls. This versatility transforms voice assistants into invaluable personal assistants, streamlining daily tasks and enhancing productivity.

Privacy and security are important considerations when using voice assistants. Most voice assistants employ encryption and secure data storage to protect your personal information. You can also manage privacy settings and control the level of data sharing within the associated apps or settings. It's essential to review and understand the privacy policies and practices of the voice assistant and associated devices to ensure a secure and comfortable user experience.

Setting up voice assistants and smart speakers is typically a straightforward process. Follow the manufacturer's instructions to connect the device to your home network, download the associated app, and complete the setup. Once configured, you can begin enjoying the convenience of voice-activated control and the multitude of services and features offered by the voice assistant.

By incorporating voice assistants and smart speakers into your smart home setup, you can experience a new level of convenience, accessibility, and personalization. The subsequent sections of this book will explore other aspects of enhancing comfort and convenience, delving into additional device categories and their integration within a smart home ecosystem. Get ready to unleash the power of voice control and enjoy a truly hands-free and intelligent living environment.

B. Smart appliances and automated routines

Smart appliances are revolutionizing the way we interact with our home appliances, offering enhanced convenience, efficiency, and automation. These intelligent devices can be seamlessly integrated into your smart home ecosystem, allowing you to control and manage them with ease.

One of the key benefits of smart appliances is their ability to provide remote control and monitoring capabilities. Through smartphone apps or centralized hubs, you can remotely adjust settings, monitor usage, and receive notifications about the status of your appliances. For example, you can preheat your oven on your way home or check if you left the refrigerator door open while you're at work.

Smart appliances also offer automation features that can simplify daily routines and save time. You can create automated routines or schedules to ensure your appliances operate at optimal times and settings. For instance, you can schedule your washing machine to start a load of laundry during off-peak hours, taking advantage of lower energy costs. You can also program your coffee maker to start brewing your favorite cup of coffee when you wake up in the morning.

Integration with voice assistants and smart home hubs allows for voice-activated control of your smart appliances. With a simple voice command, you can turn on your smart TV, adjust the temperature on your smart oven, or even start a robotic vacuum cleaner. This hands-free control adds convenience and simplifies your interaction with appliances, making daily tasks more efficient and enjoyable.

Smart appliances often feature advanced energy-saving capabilities, helping to reduce energy consumption and lower utility bills. For example, smart refrigerators can optimize cooling based on the contents and usage patterns, reducing energy waste. Smart thermostats can work in tandem with smart appliances, coordinating energy usage to maximize efficiency. These energy-saving features contribute to a more sustainable and eco-friendly home environment.

Many smart appliances provide valuable insights and analytics about energy usage and consumption patterns. With this information, you can make informed decisions to further optimize efficiency and reduce energy waste. You can identify energy-intensive appliances, track usage trends, and make adjustments to save energy and lower costs.

When selecting smart appliances, consider compatibility with your existing smart home infrastructure. Ensure that the appliances can integrate seamlessly with your smart home hub or controller. Look for devices that support common protocols such as Wi-Fi, Zigbee, or Z-Wave. Compatibility allows for centralized control and coordination of your smart appliances within your smart home ecosystem.

It's important to consider the reliability and reputation of the appliance manufacturer. Read product reviews and customer feedback to gauge the performance and durability of the appliances. Look for energy-efficient certifications and labels to ensure that the appliances meet the necessary standards for energy efficiency.

The installation and setup of smart appliances may vary depending on the type and model. Follow the manufacturer's instructions for proper installation and connectivity. Some appliances may require professional installation, particularly if they involve complex wiring or integration with existing systems.

By incorporating smart appliances and automated routines into your smart home setup, you can experience increased convenience, efficiency, and control over your daily tasks. The subsequent sections of this book will explore other aspects of enhancing comfort and convenience, delving into additional device categories and their integration within a smart home ecosystem. Get ready to simplify your life with smart appliances and automated routines that transform your living space into a truly intelligent and efficient home.

C. Entertainment systems and media integration

Entertainment systems play a vital role in transforming living spaces into immersive and enjoyable environments. With the integration of smart devices and media systems, you can create a seamless and personalized entertainment experience that caters to your preferences and enhances your comfort and convenience.

One of the key components of entertainment systems is the integration of smart TVs or streaming devices. These devices offer a wide range of streaming options, allowing you to access your favorite movies, TV shows, music, and online content with ease. Smart TVs and streaming devices often come with built-in apps or support popular streaming platforms such as Netflix, Hulu, or Spotify. With just a few clicks or voice commands, you can enjoy a vast library of entertainment options directly from your living room.

Integration with voice assistants further enhances the convenience of entertainment systems. With voice commands, you can search for specific movies or shows, control playback, adjust volume, or even switch between different apps or streaming services. Voice control eliminates the need for multiple remote controls or complex menu navigation, making it effortless to access your preferred entertainment at any time.

Smart speakers and sound systems are crucial components of media integration within a smart home. These devices offer high-quality audio and can be synchronized with your entertainment systems for immersive sound experiences. With smart speakers, you can stream music, create multi-room audio setups, or even control your entertainment systems using voice commands. The ability to integrate sound systems with other smart devices, such as lighting or security systems, adds an extra layer of immersion and creates synchronized experiences.

Smart home integration extends to media storage and management as well. With network-attached storage (NAS) devices or cloud-based services, you can store and organize your media library, including movies, TV shows, music, and photos. This centralized storage allows for easy access to your media from multiple devices, ensuring a seamless and consistent experience across different platforms.

Automation routines can enhance the entertainment experience by creating personalized scenes or settings. For instance, you can set up an automation routine that dims the lights, adjusts the temperature, and starts playing your favorite music or movie when you say a specific phrase or enter a designated area. These automated routines can turn your living space into a home theater or create a cozy ambiance for a relaxing evening.

Home theater systems provide the ultimate entertainment experience, delivering high-quality audio and immersive visuals. With smart home integration, you can control your home theater setup using voice commands or smartphone apps. From adjusting audio settings to managing lighting effects, you have full control over the atmosphere and media playback, providing an unparalleled cinematic experience in the comfort of your own home.

It's important to ensure that your entertainment systems and media devices are compatible with your smart home infrastructure. Check for compatibility with popular protocols such as Wi-Fi, Bluetooth, or Chromecast to ensure seamless integration. Research and select devices that offer the features and functionalities you desire, whether it's 4K resolution, Dolby Atmos sound, or support for your preferred streaming services.

Proper installation and setup of entertainment systems may require professional assistance, especially for complex configurations or home theater installations. Consult experts or follow manufacturer guidelines to ensure optimal performance and functionality.

By integrating entertainment systems and media devices within your smart home, you can create personalized and immersive experiences that enhance your comfort and enjoyment. The subsequent sections of this book will explore other aspects of enhancing comfort and convenience, delving into additional device categories and their integration within a smart home ecosystem. Get ready to elevate your entertainment experience and transform your living space into a hub of multimedia enjoyment.

CHAPTER VII
Managing Your Smart Home

A. Setting up and customizing automation

Automation is one of the key features that make a smart home truly intelligent and convenient. By setting up and customizing automation routines, you can streamline daily tasks, enhance efficiency, and create personalized experiences tailored to your preferences and lifestyle.

The first step in setting up automation is identifying the tasks or actions you want to automate. Consider routine activities such as turning on/off lights, adjusting thermostat settings, locking doors, or even starting your coffee maker in the morning. By automating these tasks, you can save time and effort while enjoying a more seamless and convenient living experience.

Most smart home systems or hubs come with dedicated automation features and interfaces that allow you to create custom routines. These interfaces are typically user-friendly and intuitive, providing options to select triggers, actions, and conditions for each automation routine. Triggers can be based on specific times, events, or even sensor inputs. Actions are the tasks you want to automate, such as turning on lights or adjusting temperatures. Conditions allow you to set criteria that must be met for the automation to activate, adding flexibility and customization.

Consider your daily routines and habits when creating automation routines. For example, you can set up a routine that turns off all the lights, locks the doors, and lowers the thermostat when you leave the house. Alternatively, you can schedule the blinds to open gradually in the morning to simulate a natural sunrise and wake you up gently. By aligning automation with your daily activities, you can create a more intuitive and personalized smart home experience.

Integration with voice assistants further enhances the customization and control of automation routines. Voice commands can activate specific routines or trigger customized actions, allowing for hands-free control and seamless interaction with your smart home. For instance, you can say, "Goodnight," and have your voice assistant activate a routine that turns off all the lights, adjusts the thermostat, and sets the security system to nighttime mode.

Regularly review and fine-tune your automation routines to ensure they align with your changing needs and preferences. As your routines evolve, you may discover new tasks or actions that can be automated for further convenience. Additionally, take advantage of the flexibility offered by your smart home system to adjust conditions, triggers, or actions based on seasonal changes or special events.

It's important to strike a balance between automation and manual control. While automation can greatly simplify daily tasks, it's essential to retain manual control when needed. Ensure that you have the ability to override or adjust automated routines as circumstances dictate. This ensures that you remain in control of your smart home and can make immediate changes when necessary.

When setting up automation, consider the security and privacy implications. Take precautions to secure your smart home network, use strong passwords, and regularly update firmware and software. Review the privacy settings and permissions of your smart home devices and systems to ensure that your personal information and data are protected.

By setting up and customizing automation routines, you can create a smart home environment that caters to your preferences, simplifies daily tasks, and enhances efficiency. The subsequent sections of this book will explore other aspects of managing your smart home, delving into additional features and considerations to optimize your smart home experience. Get ready to unlock the full potential of automation and customization as you take control of your smart home.

B. Monitoring and troubleshooting common issues

As with any complex system, smart homes may encounter occasional issues or glitches. Being able to monitor and troubleshoot these common issues is essential for maintaining the optimal performance and functionality of your smart home. By staying vigilant and addressing problems promptly, you can ensure a seamless and enjoyable smart home experience.

Regularly monitoring your smart home devices and systems is crucial to catch any potential issues early on. Keep an eye on device notifications, alerts, or error messages that may indicate problems. Many smart home systems or apps provide dashboards or status updates that allow you to monitor the connectivity and operation of your devices. By regularly checking these indicators, you can proactively identify and address any issues before they escalate.

Network connectivity is a common source of problems in smart homes. Ensure that all your devices are properly connected to your home network and have a stable and reliable internet connection. Weak or inconsistent Wi-Fi signals can cause devices to disconnect or experience delays in response. Consider using Wi-Fi extenders or mesh networks to improve coverage and eliminate dead zones within your home.

Firmware and software updates are critical for maintaining the security and performance of your smart home devices. Regularly check for updates and apply them promptly. Updates often include bug fixes, security patches, and performance enhancements that address common issues. Most smart home systems or devices have automatic update features that you can enable to ensure you stay up-to-date effortlessly.

If you encounter specific issues with individual devices, consult the user manual or online support resources provided by the manufacturer. Many common issues have simple solutions that can be found through troubleshooting guides or FAQs. If necessary, reach out to customer support for assistance or further troubleshooting guidance. They can often provide valuable insights and recommendations specific to your device or system.

It's essential to maintain good device hygiene and ensure that devices are clean and free from physical obstructions. Dust, debris, or other particles can interfere with device sensors or components, leading to performance issues. Regularly clean your devices following manufacturer guidelines to keep them in optimal condition.

Password management and security practices are crucial for protecting your smart home from potential threats. Change default passwords on your devices and use strong, unique passwords for each device and online account. Regularly review and update passwords to mitigate the risk of unauthorized access. Consider enabling additional security features such as two-factor authentication or encryption to enhance the security of your smart home.

It's advisable to keep a record of your smart home setup, including device models, serial numbers, and any relevant configuration details. This documentation can be useful for troubleshooting or seeking assistance from customer support. Additionally, maintaining a backup of your smart home settings or configurations can help expedite the recovery process in case of a system reset or device failure.

By actively monitoring your smart home devices, staying up-to-date with firmware and software updates, and promptly addressing any issues that arise, you can ensure the smooth operation and longevity of your smart home. The subsequent sections of this book will explore other aspects of managing your smart home, delving into additional features and considerations to optimize your smart home experience. Get ready to be a proactive manager of your smart home and enjoy the benefits of a seamless and hassle-free living environment.

C. Data privacy and security concerns

In the age of interconnected devices, data privacy and security are paramount considerations for managing your smart home. As smart home technology collects and processes personal information, it's essential to take steps to safeguard your data and protect your privacy. By being proactive and implementing best practices, you can enjoy the benefits of a smart home while maintaining control over your personal information.

Start by reviewing the privacy policies and terms of service for your smart home devices and systems. Understand how your data is collected, stored, and shared by the manufacturers and service providers. Look for clear and transparent policies that prioritize user privacy and offer options to control data sharing and permissions.

Protecting your smart home network is crucial for data privacy and security. Secure your home Wi-Fi network with a strong password and enable encryption. Regularly update your router's firmware to patch any security vulnerabilities. Consider creating a separate network specifically for your smart home devices to isolate them from your main network and other connected devices.

When setting up your smart home devices, avoid using default usernames and passwords. Change the default credentials to unique, strong passwords for each device.

Additionally, enable any available security features such as two-factor authentication to add an extra layer of protection against unauthorized access.

Regularly update the firmware and software of your smart home devices and systems. Manufacturers often release updates that address security vulnerabilities or improve device performance. Enable automatic updates whenever possible to ensure that you stay up-to-date with the latest security patches and enhancements.

Pay attention to the permissions and access requests made by smart home apps or devices. Only grant necessary permissions and consider limiting access to sensitive data. For example, if an app requests access to your contacts or location data but does not require it for its functionality, consider denying that permission.

Keep track of the devices connected to your smart home ecosystem. Disconnect any devices that are no longer in use or that you no longer trust. Regularly review the list of connected devices and remove any unfamiliar or suspicious devices that you don't recognize. This helps ensure that only authorized devices have access to your smart home network.

Consider using a virtual private network (VPN) when accessing your smart home remotely. A VPN encrypts your internet connection, providing an additional layer of security when accessing your smart home devices or monitoring systems outside your home. This helps protect your data from potential eavesdropping or unauthorized access.

Educate yourself and your family members about smart home security and privacy best practices. Promote good habits such as avoiding clicking on suspicious links or downloading unverified apps. Encourage strong password management and the use of unique credentials for each smart home device or online account.

Lastly, regularly review the privacy settings and options provided by your smart home devices and apps. Adjust these settings to align with your privacy preferences and comfort level. Consider disabling any features or data sharing options that you are not comfortable with, and regularly review and update these settings as needed.

By implementing these data privacy and security measures, you can enjoy the convenience and benefits of a smart home while safeguarding your personal information. The subsequent sections of this book will explore other aspects of managing your smart home, delving into additional features and considerations to optimize your smart home experience. Get ready to prioritize data privacy and security as you manage and enjoy the full potential of your smart home.

CHAPTER VIII
The Future of Smart Homes

A. Emerging technologies and trends

The world of smart homes is constantly evolving, and exciting emerging technologies are shaping the future of this industry. As we look ahead, several trends and innovations hold promise for further enhancing the capabilities and functionality of smart homes. Let's explore some of these emerging technologies that are set to transform the way we live.

❖ Artificial Intelligence (AI) - AI is playing a pivotal role in the advancement of smart homes. With AI-powered devices and algorithms, smart home systems can learn and adapt to our preferences and behaviors, making our living spaces more intuitive and personalized. AI-driven assistants can anticipate our needs, automate routine tasks, and provide proactive suggestions to enhance our comfort and convenience.

❖ Internet of Things (IoT) Expansion - The Internet of Things continues to expand, with more devices becoming interconnected and capable of sharing data. This growth paves the way for greater integration and seamless communication among smart home devices. From smart appliances to wearables, the expanding IoT ecosystem enables a more comprehensive and interconnected smart home experience.

❖ Voice and Gesture Recognition - Voice and gesture recognition technologies are becoming increasingly sophisticated, enabling more intuitive and natural interactions with smart home devices. Improved speech recognition algorithms and voice assistants allow for more accurate voice commands and context-based responses. Similarly, advancements in gesture recognition technology enable touchless control of devices, making interactions more effortless and hygienic.

❖ Augmented Reality (AR) and Virtual Reality (VR) - AR and VR technologies have the potential to revolutionize the way we experience and interact with our smart homes. With AR, we can overlay virtual information onto our physical environment, providing real-time feedback and enhancing our understanding and control of smart devices. VR, on the other hand, can transport us to immersive virtual environments, creating unique entertainment and simulation experiences within our smart homes.

❖ Energy Harvesting and Sustainability - As sustainability becomes increasingly important, smart homes are adopting energy harvesting technologies to improve efficiency and reduce environmental impact. Energy harvesting devices can convert ambient energy sources such as solar, kinetic, or thermal energy into usable power for smart home devices. This trend promotes self-sufficiency and contributes to a greener and more sustainable future.

❖ Robotics and Automation - The integration of robotics and automation technologies is set to revolutionize the functionality and capabilities of smart homes. From robotic vacuum cleaners to automated home security systems, these technologies enhance convenience, efficiency, and safety within our living spaces. As robotic capabilities advance, we can expect to see more sophisticated and versatile robots that assist with various tasks around the home.

❖ Data Analytics and Personalization - With the increasing amount of data generated by smart home devices, data analytics and machine learning algorithms enable valuable insights and personalized experiences. By analyzing usage patterns, preferences, and environmental factors, smart home systems can adapt and optimize settings to create a tailored and comfortable living environment for each individual.

❖ Enhanced Security and Privacy Measures - As smart homes become more prevalent, there is a growing emphasis on robust security and privacy measures. Manufacturers are investing in encryption technologies, secure protocols, and privacy features to protect personal data and prevent unauthorized access. The future of smart homes will see even more sophisticated security measures to ensure the safety and privacy of occupants.

These emerging technologies and trends indicate an exciting future for smart homes. As innovation continues, we can expect further integration, personalization, and automation within our living spaces. The subsequent sections of this book will explore other aspects of the future of smart homes, delving into additional possibilities and considerations as we embrace these transformative technologies. Get ready to embark on an exciting journey into the future of smart homes and experience a new level of comfort, convenience, and connectivity.

B. Integration with Internet of Things (IoT)

The Internet of Things (IoT) continues to expand and evolve, and its integration with smart homes holds immense potential for transforming the way we live. As the number of interconnected devices increases, the seamless integration of IoT within smart homes will further enhance their functionality, connectivity, and efficiency. Let's explore some of the exciting possibilities and benefits of this integration.

- ❖ Comprehensive Connectivity - The integration of IoT within smart homes enables comprehensive connectivity among various devices and systems. From smart appliances to lighting, security systems, and entertainment devices, the IoT ecosystem allows for seamless communication, coordination, and control. This interconnectedness facilitates intelligent automation, where devices work together to optimize settings, conserve energy, and enhance the overall living experience.

- ❖ Data Sharing and Insights - The IoT integration enables devices to share data and collaborate, leading to valuable insights and optimizations. For example, sensors within smart homes can collect data on temperature, occupancy, lighting, and energy usage. This data can then be analyzed to identify patterns, optimize energy consumption, and provide actionable insights for improving efficiency and comfort within the home.

❖ Contextual Awareness - IoT integration enhances the contextual awareness of smart home devices. By sharing data and leveraging machine learning algorithms, devices can understand the occupants' preferences, habits, and environmental conditions. For instance, lighting systems can adjust brightness and color temperature based on natural light levels or occupants' activities. Smart thermostats can optimize temperature settings based on occupancy and weather forecasts. This contextual awareness leads to personalized and intuitive experiences that adapt to individual needs.

❖ Intelligent Automation - With the integration of IoT, smart homes can achieve a higher level of intelligent automation. Devices can collaborate and automate routine tasks based on predefined rules, sensor inputs, or occupant preferences. For example, when a motion sensor detects no occupancy in a room, it can automatically turn off lights and adjust the temperature to save energy. The integration with IoT enables complex automation scenarios, making our living spaces more convenient, efficient, and responsive.

❖ Interoperability and Compatibility - As the IoT ecosystem expands, efforts are being made to establish interoperability and compatibility standards. These standards aim to ensure that devices from different manufacturers can seamlessly work together within a smart home environment. The integration with IoT fosters a diverse and interoperable ecosystem, allowing users to choose from a wide range of devices and systems that suit their preferences and needs.

❖ Voice Control and Smart Assistants - IoT integration enhances voice control capabilities and smart assistant functionalities within smart homes. Voice commands can be used to control and interact with various IoT devices, such as adjusting lighting, playing music, or managing home security systems.

The integration of IoT expands the scope of voice control, enabling more comprehensive and intuitive interactions with our smart homes.

❖ Real-Time Monitoring and Remote Access - IoT integration enables real-time monitoring and remote access to smart home devices and systems. With IoT-enabled sensors and connectivity, users can monitor and control their homes remotely, ensuring peace of mind and control even when away. Whether it's checking security camera feeds, adjusting thermostat settings, or receiving alerts, the integration with IoT provides the flexibility and convenience of remote access.

❖ Evolving Possibilities - As the IoT landscape evolves, we can expect further advancements and possibilities within smart homes. The integration of emerging technologies such as 5G, edge computing, and blockchain can enhance the speed, reliability, and security of IoT devices and systems. This opens doors to exciting new applications and services that will further revolutionize our living spaces.

The integration of IoT within smart homes promises a future of seamless connectivity, intelligent automation, and personalized experiences. The subsequent sections of this book will explore other aspects of the future of smart homes, delving into additional possibilities and considerations as we embrace the integration with IoT. Get ready to embark on an exciting journey into the future of smart homes and experience a new level of connectivity, efficiency, and convenience.

C. Potential challenges and future possibilities

As smart homes continue to evolve, they bring forth a range of possibilities and potential challenges that shape the future of this technology. While the benefits of smart homes are vast, it's important to consider the challenges that may arise and explore how future advancements can overcome these hurdles. Let's delve into some of the potential challenges and future possibilities that lie ahead.

❖ Interoperability and Standardization - One of the challenges in the realm of smart homes is the lack of interoperability and standardization among devices and platforms. As the number of smart home devices increases, ensuring compatibility and seamless integration between different brands and protocols becomes crucial. Future advancements may include the establishment of industry standards and protocols, allowing devices from various manufacturers to communicate and work together seamlessly.

❖ Privacy and Data Security - With the growing number of connected devices and the collection of personal data, privacy and data security are vital concerns. Protecting sensitive information and ensuring secure communication between devices are ongoing challenges. Future advancements may involve enhanced encryption methods, stricter privacy regulations, and user-friendly tools for managing data permissions and access control. Continued efforts in strengthening security measures will be pivotal to building trust in smart home technology.

❖ Energy Efficiency and Sustainability - While smart homes offer energy-saving capabilities, future possibilities lie in further optimizing energy efficiency and embracing sustainable practices. Advancements may include integrating renewable energy sources, such as solar panels or home energy storage systems, to power smart home devices. Additionally, more sophisticated energy management algorithms and machine learning models can be developed to analyze energy usage patterns and suggest further improvements, contributing to a greener and more sustainable future.

❖ User Experience and Interface Design - The user experience and interface design play crucial roles in the widespread adoption and acceptance of smart homes. Simplifying the setup process, improving device discoverability, and enhancing user interfaces will make smart home technology more accessible to a broader audience. Future possibilities include intuitive interfaces, natural language processing, and augmented reality (AR) overlays to enhance user interactions and make smart homes more user-friendly and inclusive.

❖ Cost and Affordability - Affordability remains a barrier for many individuals seeking to adopt smart home technology. The cost of devices, installation, and infrastructure can limit the accessibility and widespread adoption of smart homes. Future possibilities involve advancements in manufacturing processes, economies of scale, and increased competition, which can drive down costs and make smart home technology more affordable for a larger portion of the population.

❖ Artificial Intelligence and Machine Learning - The integration of artificial intelligence (AI) and machine learning (ML) holds immense potential for smart homes. Future advancements in AI and ML algorithms can enable more advanced automation, intelligent decision-making, and predictive analytics within smart home systems. These technologies will continually learn and adapt to occupants' preferences, habits, and environmental factors, creating even more personalized and intuitive experiences.

❖ Health and Well-being - Smart homes have the potential to contribute to occupant health and well-being. Future possibilities include the integration of health-monitoring devices, such as wearable fitness trackers or medical sensors, into smart home ecosystems. These devices can provide real-time health data, monitor sleep patterns, and help create personalized environments that promote better health and well-being.

❖ Social and Ethical Implications - As smart homes become more prevalent, there are social and ethical implications that need consideration. Issues such as data privacy, algorithm bias, and the digital divide should be addressed to ensure equitable access, fairness, and transparency in smart home technology. Future advancements may involve the development of guidelines, regulations, and ethical frameworks to navigate these complex challenges and foster responsible innovation.

While challenges exist, the future possibilities for smart homes are vast. Through continued research, innovation, and collaboration, we can overcome hurdles and unlock the full potential of this technology. The subsequent sections of this book will explore other aspects of the future of smart homes, delving into additional possibilities and considerations. Get ready to embrace the future possibilities and shape the smart homes of tomorrow.

Conclusion

A. Recap of key points

In this book, we have explored the fascinating world of smart homes and how they are revolutionizing our living spaces. Let's recap the key points we have covered throughout this journey.

We began by understanding the importance of the home environment and how smart home technology is transforming it. The rise of smart home technology has brought about numerous benefits and advantages, debunking common misconceptions along the way.

Getting started with smart home technology involves assessing your current living space, planning and budgeting for a smart home setup, and carefully choosing the right devices and systems that align with your needs and preferences.

Smart home integration plays a crucial role in connecting devices and creating a network that allows for seamless communication and control. Smart home hubs and controllers serve as centralized command centers, while choosing the right devices and systems ensures compatibility and optimal functionality within your smart home ecosystem.

Transforming living spaces involves leveraging smart lighting and ambiance control to create personalized environments. Energy efficiency and smart thermostats contribute to a greener and more cost-effective home, while home security and surveillance systems provide peace of mind and protect your loved ones.

Enhancing comfort and convenience includes the integration of voice assistants and smart speakers, as well as utilizing smart appliances and automated routines to simplify daily tasks and save time.

Managing your smart home involves setting up and customizing automation routines to streamline your daily routines and personalizing your smart home experience. Monitoring and troubleshooting common issues ensure optimal performance and functionality, while being mindful of data privacy and security concerns protects your personal information.

Finally, we explored the future of smart homes, including emerging technologies and trends such as the integration with the Internet of Things (IoT). We discussed the potential challenges and future possibilities, such as interoperability, privacy and security, energy efficiency, user experience, and the integration of artificial intelligence.

As we conclude this book, it is evident that smart homes have the potential to transform our lives, making them more comfortable, convenient, and efficient. The future of smart homes is bright, with advancements on the horizon that will continue to enhance our living experiences.

By embracing smart home technology, considering the key points discussed in this book, and staying open to future possibilities, you can embark on a journey to transform your living space into a truly intelligent and connected home.

Now it's up to you to take the knowledge and insights gained from this book and embark on your own smart home revolution. Enjoy the journey and the endless possibilities that await you in your smart home!

B. Encouragement for readers to embrace the smart home revolution

As we come to the end of this book, I want to take a moment to encourage you to embrace the smart home revolution and embark on an exciting journey of transforming your living space. The possibilities and benefits that smart homes offer are truly remarkable, and by embracing this revolution, you can elevate your lifestyle and create a living environment that is tailored to your needs and preferences.

Embracing the smart home revolution means stepping into a world where convenience, efficiency, and comfort seamlessly intertwine. Imagine walking into a home that knows your preferences, adjusts the lighting and temperature just the way you like it, and welcomes you with your favorite music playing softly in the background. With smart home technology, this can become a reality.

By embracing the smart home revolution, you open the door to a new level of control and automation. Routine tasks can be automated, freeing up your time and energy for more meaningful activities. You can effortlessly manage your energy consumption, reducing your environmental impact and saving on utility bills. Smart security systems offer enhanced protection for your home and loved ones, providing peace of mind even when you're away.

The smart home revolution is not just about gadgets and technology; it's about creating a living space that truly reflects your personality and enhances your lifestyle. It's about personalization and customization, where your home adapts to your needs and preferences. With the integration of smart devices and systems, you have the power to create an environment that is uniquely yours.

While embracing the smart home revolution may initially seem overwhelming, remember that every journey begins with a single step. Start by assessing your current living space and identifying areas where smart home technology can make a difference. Set a budget and prioritize the devices and systems that align with your goals and interests. Take your time to research and choose the right solutions that meet your needs.

Embracing the smart home revolution also means being open to learning and adapting. The world of smart homes is constantly evolving, with new technologies and advancements on the horizon. Stay curious, explore new possibilities, and be willing to experiment with different devices and systems. Embrace the learning process and enjoy the satisfaction of discovering new ways to enhance your smart home experience.

Remember, the smart home revolution is not just about the technology itself; it's about the lifestyle it enables. It's about simplifying your daily routines, enhancing your comfort and convenience, and creating a living space that reflects your personality and values. So, embrace the smart home revolution with enthusiasm and curiosity, and let it transform your living space into a place you're proud to call home.

Thank you for joining me on this journey of exploring the smart home revolution. I hope this book has provided you with valuable insights and inspiration to embark on your own smart home adventure. Embrace the possibilities, embrace the convenience, and embrace the future of smart homes. Your journey starts now!

C. Final thoughts and closing remarks

As we reach the end of this book, I would like to share some final thoughts and offer closing remarks on the smart home revolution that we have explored together.

Smart homes have truly transformed the way we live, offering a plethora of benefits and possibilities. They have revolutionized our living spaces, providing us with unprecedented control, convenience, and comfort. The integration of technology, automation, and connectivity has given rise to an intelligent ecosystem that adapts to our needs and enhances our daily lives.

Throughout this book, we have discussed the importance of the home environment and the rise of smart home technology. We have explored the purpose of this book, which is to guide you through understanding smart homes, getting started with smart home technology, integrating devices and systems, transforming living spaces, enhancing comfort and convenience, managing your smart home, and envisioning the future of smart homes.

Along the way, we have covered various topics, including the definition and components of smart homes, the benefits and advantages they offer, common misconceptions, assessing your living space, planning and budgeting, choosing the right devices and systems, connecting devices and creating networks, transforming lighting and ambiance, optimizing energy efficiency, ensuring home security, utilizing voice assistants and smart speakers, embracing smart appliances and automated routines, integrating entertainment systems, setting up automation, monitoring and troubleshooting common issues, and addressing data privacy and security concerns.

We have also discussed the future of smart homes, exploring emerging technologies, trends, potential challenges, and future possibilities, such as the integration with the Internet of Things (IoT), and the importance of embracing this revolution.

As you embark on your smart home journey, remember that the most important aspect is your vision for your living space. Let your imagination guide you as you create a smart home that aligns with your unique preferences, needs, and aspirations. Embrace the opportunities to simplify your life, save energy, enhance security, and personalize your living environment.

However, as with any technological advancement, it is crucial to remain mindful of potential challenges and stay informed about best practices in data privacy, security, and responsible use of smart home technology. By adopting a proactive and informed approach, you can ensure a safe, secure, and enjoyable smart home experience.

The smart home revolution is an ongoing journey. As technology continues to evolve and new innovations emerge, the possibilities for smart homes will only expand. Embrace the excitement of this ever-changing landscape and stay open to future advancements and possibilities.

I hope this book has provided you with a comprehensive understanding of smart homes and the tools to embark on your own smart home revolution. Whether you are just starting your smart home journey or looking to expand and optimize your existing setup, remember that the true essence of a smart home lies in creating a living space that reflects your unique lifestyle, values, and aspirations.

Thank you for joining me on this exploration of the smart home revolution. May your smart home bring you comfort, convenience, and joy as it transforms your living space into a haven perfectly tailored to your needs.

Embrace the possibilities, embrace the technology, and embrace the future of smart homes. Your journey begins now.

www.ingramcontent.com/pod-product-compliance
Lightning Source LLC
LaVergne TN
LVHW022125060326
832903LV00063B/4115